POEMS

POEMS

c.marie

VANTAGE PRESS
New York

Contents

POEMS

Fall

Loose leaf binder
Hangs on a stem.
Snap rings hold it together.
Hung in the moment,
Flung back and forth
In the wind.

This quiet container
Filled to the brim
Lands when the leaf's fall ends.

a.m.

In a
Forest fawn dark,
On a silent frost lawn,
Crisp frosted flakes
Starts the morning rush buzz.
Flying with corner cup
Steam rising to sigh
Through my lips.
Again to the finish
Round off the last sip
To breathe in
The rest of the day.

Garnish

Light on the side
Of my greenery,
Shaded by leaves
Round the rim.
Soft swirl sips
Pour through my lips
As beads of life
Fall adrift.

So

So puffed up and popular
So full of self
Plucked at others' expense.

Using is useful
To stuff the chest
Full to the brim
With self credit.

So important to be
The hive that is seen,
And be the bee
Lost in their bonnet.

Sweet

Treat the world
Sweet.
A savored taste
Released.

A flavor
Unfolding
Layers of senses
Making it new
Every second.

Molding
Many molecular moments together
Connecting life
Sweet.

I

A ladybug landed on my windshield
With a grip against the wind.
Such tiny strength
            In microscopic limbs
            Hung on.

Taking flight with a force
            To carry on its wings
That blew through elements
Beyond itself,
Until it met an end,

In its next
Close touch land again.

II

Once or twice
Was lost the chance
To catch a moment freed.

To breathe in deep
And let life pass
To the next cog in the wheel.

The plan has passed
The end is gone
Onto another space.

And in this second
Chance is where
A moment
Found
Its place.

Wish Mist

Foggy mist day
Slow to fulfill
Time to make
Light of the day.

Yet softer the seconds
Go soaking in steps
To lift up the night
On its way.

Slow groggy the haze
Passing over the sun
To greet the last moon
From its cave.

Rolling on motion
Settles the course
Hiding the light
Of the day.

But in its own moment
Covered in time,
Light's found hanging
In the night's mind.

Snag

A snag in the fabric
Of life
A gather
Pulled a ripple
Too tight.
Tugging the wayward thread
Pressing it smooth
Firm is the plan
To restore
It new again.

III

When broken
Severed lines
Are drawn.
And forever wedges
Sown.
Leaving only
One to watch
The end

Going farther
From the shore

Farther from once more.

The Last Hour

The last hour
		Is always longer
The clicking minutes
		Stall.
The final moment
		Is put off
Until it has to call.

And when the second makes
		Its mark
And the time has come.

The long-awaited
		Light is there

For longing further on.

IV

When
A turning point second
Fork in the road
Split into possible chances.

Where
Weaving the ends
Ends over ends
Set into motion again.
Again and again
Layers land
Unfolding the next lines in the yarn.

Pulling it tight
Tied in a knot
To finish
     the end
       once again.

Jet Stream

Jet streams spred
Along an ocean sky
A foam life coats
The miles.
Wider still
Where highs unseen,
Lie beyond
The ribbons
In the stream.

Hummingbird

The humming stopped.
The bird was still.
A moment
And then it flew.

Its color coat
Cast to see
A much brighter view
Beneath.

To take its flight
Fully in
Is to keep
Its sight unseen.

V

The steel trap attack
Lures you with alarm
Caught and left to fend
Alone
This unknown hinge
Snaps back.

Provoked and proven
Wrong somehow
What's only known
To bend.

The wire with a hidden coil
Beyond the reach to know
Where
The final catch is found.

VI

In an accidental moment
A slip of raveled time
Slight yet sinking
Catching on
Just in the nick of . . .

Hitting it on the fly
Running by
An early landing.

War

Every type of skin bleeds.
Blood is red for everyone.
Piercing through the
Layers of life
Hurts all.

Bleeding leads
To final places
Set in stone
Forever.

Grieving makes
It real
For the long ending to
Blood's setting.

VII

Hillside arms
In a quilted calm
Held up the clouded sky.

Rounded rolling mounds
In flight from a winded
Crestline haul.

Formed in every element
Sculpted by open air.
The floating mountains sigh
To call the hillside's
Friend to fall.

Stress

Twitching eye
Tremor buried within
Surfaces tension inside.

Telegraph signals
Code this jitter
To track
A message
Hidden within.

This invisible world listens
In absence of sight
Where detection of life
Must be sought.

Decyphering down
Underneath
Silent skin
Reveals the real
Light switch on.

End of Day

Late afternoon clarity
Sharpens the view
It's all done
In the silhouette sky.

Let go the day now.
It's burned in the sun.
Sunk in salt water
Down under the sand.

The Drive

Flat city tires
Birds on a wire,
Sentinels watching the hour.

Blinking light lanes
Stream to the end
Of the endless red
Flowing

Horizon.

VIII

Second Nature
Surrender
Ingrained in the Soul
To give up
Giving up anymore.

To let empty
Be enough
To feel Whole.

Black Crows

Black Crows
>Cross my window

Two Sparrows
>Fled to reach
A tree
>Far from them and me.

So tired
>Of those arrows
>That pound
Into my back.
>Silent claws
>Bored deep.

So when a
>Golden Monarch
>Swept by this place
Where dark glass once grew,

This light sign
>Made
>Life seem
It could be fine
>Where
>Once

Black Crows flew.

Hopping Bird

A Hopping Bird mind
        Bounced
From
        Limb to limb.

Bending and lifting
        To see
Side to side
        All across the sky,

To find the right
        Leaf left landing
        To spring.

IX

The leaves
      Grew up

To cover the hillside
      Home.

The red tile roof
      Was gone.

The tender sprouts
      Filtered

The sun
      I used to see.

And now when the wind
      Waves in the breeze

To glimpse
      Past fleeting leaves,

Still nested
      There is a home

Amongst trees'
      Newest scenes.

X

The point of never knowing
    Not ever known
    Nor found.

Is living in a dark land
    Buried
    Underground.

And in this vacant space
    There holds
    An everpresent gap.

That will never have the
    Bridge
    To piece together
What will last.

XI

Point of departure
Never going back
The last of what
Was done
Before.

A searing sad
Good-bye
A forever
Separate chore is
Embedded to the core
Once more.

And when this point
Has disappeared for good
Is long gone
And past,

A space is made
In moving on
To fill the empty space.

Side Dishes

There are always pickles in life.
Little pickles
On the side.

It's hard to keep them
From draining into
The main plate of life's plan.

Script

A cigarette burned through papers
   And peeled thick layers
      Of thought.

Deeper burns
   Went down through the rest
      As a circle of smoke
        Made a ring.

The fire ring told its
   Own story,
      This tired old soul
        Was afraid.

That in this blank moment
   A thought
      Disappeared into
        Another page
          Altogether.

The Final Say

A last word.
A note to
End the end.
The list.
The emphasis,
The walk away
When done.
The look.
The sigh.
The slam
And shut.
The final . . .